CW01424525

To The Wallaces,

WHEN THE UNIVERSE CREAKS

Love,

Simon

x

When the Universe Creaks

Poems by Simon Lamb

When the Universe Creaks
Poems by Simon Lamb

First published in the UK in 2021 by Simon Lamb Creative
www.simonlambcreative.co.uk

ISBN 978-1-9162749-1-4

© Simon Lamb 2021

The poems constituting the Cathedral Sky sequence in this book were
originally published as Cathedral Sky: Poems by Simon Lamb by
Simon Lamb Creative in 2019, ISBN 978-1-9162749-0-7

Cover illustrated by Jamie Steel
www.jamiesteelgraphicdesign.co.uk

Author photo by Nigel Lamb

Typeset by the poet

Printed and bound by ImprintDigital.com
https://digital.imprint.co.uk

First Printing
2021

Contents

QUINTET

Introduction

In the final months of 2019, I was delighted to tour my first one-man poetry show around Scotland, with stops across the east and north coasts, including an evening in Edinburgh at the Scottish Poetry Library and a wonderful weekend in the warm company of the communities up in Caithness. On the opening night of the tour, deep in the windy and winding streets of St Andrews, I released my first poetry pamphlet, *Cathedral Sky*, a sequence of approx. twenty-one verses, to be read together or individually; brief brushstrokes of life and colour and hope.

In the early months of 2020, having greatly enjoyed the experience of sharing my words live with audiences of all ages, I made preparations for a second tour, this time around the west coast of the country . . . but, sadly, it never came to be. Instead, as we all know, the world was gripped in the unrelenting and seemingly unending choke of a deadly and invisible virus – and the sky that had so recently seemed so vast and wide and blue to me now played host to great grey clouds. However, in an attempt to weather the storm with continued creativity, I found a new way of engaging with audiences remotely by filming and releasing video poems inspired by the treacly times; a refusal to let the clouds blot out the entire sky.

In the middle months of 2021, with finally some sense of the world moving forward again, and with the recent selling out of my pamphlet's print run, I took the opportunity to revisit and considerably expand the publication into the product you hold in your hands today. In it, I now present five distinct sections, something of a capturing of my work over the past few years: first up is the original *Cathedral Sky* sequence, preserved, unedited; then we take a whistle-stop poetic bus tour through the pandemic with the words to my half-dozen lockdown-themed video poems; this is followed by an honest and personal short story framed on the properties of dice; next, a brand new sequence of nature poems inspired by Scotland's Year of Coasts and Waters; and, finally, a group of five standalone poems representing some other highlights of my most recent writing. One of these concluding poems, *The Working Birds*, inspired by blue tits in the back garden, won the Robert Burns World Federation's international poetry competition in 2021 – which, in these greyest of years, was something of a silver lining. These five sections are then followed by a series of notes giving further background to the poems, their creation and composition.

It is my intention that presenting all of the above in one book will allow poems to rub shoulders with poems, images to rub shoulders with images, and words to rub shoulders with words, that new sparks may light, that new creaks may sound.

Thank you for supporting my art, and whenever you choose to read this volume, blue skies or grey, I hope it gifts you a reminder that "it is the wish of wings to fly". Safe flight.

Simon Lamb
Autumn 2021

Cathedral Sky

The sky was more than on fire:

it was positively ablaze. It was as if the gods of the night had fought in the firmament, leaving nothing but spilt blood upon the canvas of heaven.

Standing alone in the driveway, staring up, it seems impossible to imagine the sky ever becoming blue again, future generations no doubt speaking of the shade known as *sky red* as fondly as they might speak of an old friend.

Captured by the sight, he abandons the slowly defrosting car in hopes of finding a further feast for the eyes.

A moment round the corner, he finds it: an endless ocean, stretched out beneath the span of the sky; and out there, at such great distance, the horizon, blacker and more ominous than ever before.

A whisper of wind wraps itself around his legs: *Come*, it says. *Come* — and so, he does, knowing that the day ahead will be as deep as the sky, as wide as the ocean, and as unknown as the faraway fold between them . . . . .

Step By Step By Step
Life's A Journey Through The Woods
Step By Step By Step

The firmness of the tarmac road gives way to an earthen flesh: the entrance to the wild woods, a path to the yet-unknown. And so he begins his journey with that first-footed *Step By Step By Step // Life's A Journey Through The Woods // Step By Step By Step* — and this is the point of no return. Almost at once, the canopy claims the sun. The sky fares little better; nothing more than mere glimpses through the leaves. But on he goes, undeterred, *Step By Step By Step // Life's A Journey Through The Woods // Step By Step By Step.* Here, the safe, familial sounds of the world are silenced, replaced by the crunch and break of the ground. In this almost-vacuum, he is both exposed and reborn. All is new to him: the air is new, his feet are new, his vision is new. His basic greens and browns blossom into shades and hues and tints that, thus far, have been a mystery. A new world full of hopeful possibilities takes root before his very being. Why did he wait till now? Why not take this path so long ago? He sighs. Ah well, he's here now, and he intends not to go back, not now this world is his, and his to explore . . . . .

it is the wish of wings
to fly

and i am a bird

and i have wings

and i will fly

time to wish the woods goodbye

watch me tear through trees
and test my feathered friends
in newborn blue that knows no ends

a glinting zip of a song
threading melody on air

delight of first flight with all to see
no night to stop play at end of day

just up and away
up and away
and away

it is the wish of wings
to fly

and i am the sky

You were the castle
The glittering citadel with towering turrets
Awaiting me upon the road
A mirage at first
An obscene reality on my meadowed journey
Through the world

I was wary
I'd never seen a castle before
Let alone be in one
But you welcomed me with your open arms
And led me to your banquet hall
With its life and music and splendoured food

& we danced & we danced & we danced   *How we danced!*
Me, the naïve traveller; you, the castle

We stroked skin by a skyhawk moon
Each kiss the bliss of an ancient tune
And song of sheer being

So why so soon did you throw down
The portcullised lock? Why? Why?
Please, throw me the key

You are the castle

A castle I want to be

Pity the bird that finally learns to

F

                      L

                                    Y

                       then hits the glass window.

              Not
only does the bird bash its head
but so too does the window get

                          saddled
                             with
                          a stain.

                                //

                       step by step by step
                  it was the wish of wings to fly
                       step by step by step

I am very lost
        for words.

I / am / very / lost.
          Four words.

I am very lost.
        [Forewords.]

I am very lost . . . . .
        Forwards?

                    //

            I didn't want to
                write this poem

           But you
                made me
                do it

           I hope you're happy

           It is not
                a good poem

                      It means nothing
                    to anyone
                          except
                              you

each note
is knife to heart

the song that once
brought me to life
now kills me with its toothened tune

I'd play you the music
but I know you never listen

sunbeams caught in fishing nets
never know their worth
shining off scales
compares not with the lush trees
and the lapping of the forest's fur
washed in water
second fiddle to the woods
and the heads of wanderers
a splash
not a flash of fauna'd fever
oh sunbeam
canopied believer

You have heard the story,
have you not? The one about the ancient pond,
undisturbed. Recall how it tells of a frog that
jumps in the pool, sounding out an almighty
s p l a s h ! — till silence fills the glade anew.

Notice how the story speaks
of silence, yes, but stillness, no.

You see, the ripple flollops outward,
upsetting all around. A water-circle
widening: A ripple! A rush! A roar!
Result: a tsunami
from the pond before.

And, I ask you, what of the frog?
And you reply:

> *The frog is old.*

> *The frog is silent.*

> *The frog is guilty.*

> *The frog is glum.*

And what of the bird?

And you reply:

> *What bird?*

Can I crumple this sky and start over?
Untack the blue and ball it up
like an idea lost and tossed aside?
Can I wipe this stratosphere clean?
Scrape away its sinewy pulses:
spaghetti hung on sky.
Can I rescue the trees that took root
in a fruitless wood? If only I could,
I'd save the plates from the crack of the storm,
keep them close, warm; and I'd take more care
with the wish of the wings, and do the things
I should have done instead of those
I could have done and did, and hid within
the clangoured din of empty, silent places,
away from faces; erase all traces
of the crinkles and the creases
of a sky that never ceases. Endless stories
keep us spinning, but I beg a new beginning.
Wings were made for flying, yes,
not taking on the sky;
I know the who and what and where
but want to learn the why,
and if blessed with starting over
then, believe me, I will try
to live a life of living
'neath a new uncrumpled sky.

How the ice of all the years
drapes itself around the harbour now
crisp and harsh and here

Silence from the bottled boats

Gulls lost upon the tide

The warmth of windowpanes
but frost and flake

Wake! Wake! Oh place of life
and glow once more

Forgive the cold and chill their wronged endeavour
blast away the wayward weather
find again your firmest tether
spread your harboured arms
and give each boat
its place to float
forever

— the maker's masterwork hangs above my head
and solemn, sun-soaked years
seem to swirl in a great vortex between us
carving out a channel
from the here and now
to the there and then
from the poet's hand
to the hands of them that built it all
designing and fleshing
such stories of stories
in colour and life
through sweat and strife
a teased-out tapestry of time itself
beneath / beyond the sky

— and then a paint drop drips
through the ongoing faith of the universe
landing in my outstretched palm
enriching me by its fall
through nothing and everything

— and in that moment
that briefest blink of a moment
I understand:
history is a self creation
never fully finished
so too am I

I will not let Fear be my permanent address.

Instead I'll pave:
a boulevard of hope
an avenue of dreams
and a sidewalk of possibility.

All may walk there,
especially those who live in Fear.

by blade

by grain

by foam

by sky

by stars

I'll paint a new world

and it shall be a good world

untroubled except

for the bristles

and the choke

of the artist's mind

and in it we'll find

life

the scene shifts

the overstory crumbles

the light returns

and halfway through a holloway
a single feather   flutters

O my gentle raider:
see the stones you've stolen in your shoes.
Did you leave any on the path?

Come, gouge them from your sole.
Prise each painful pebble from the grooves
and thumb their sharpest edges down.

Heap them here, all of them.
Ah, it seems you have a mountain too.
Ascend this rocky road you've built

and know each step is made
on top of all that came before you:
felled trees and broken wings as well.

Oh, how light you must feel
after setting down a mountainside.
Please, leave it here and journey on.

Ignore its cracking crust.
Pass by its bursting buds. Let go.
The mountain is no longer yours.

Concern yourself with now.
Spread your arms beneath the sanguine sky
and to the wild wind proclaim:

I came. I came.

The snow shards sprinkled down from the sky,
                                        drifting,
                                                sifting
through the early evening air.
                        Welly boots
                                sploshed
                                        through the
slushy scene,
                excited, eager, keen.
                                Sledges sliced
                                        down slippy
slopes,
        soundtracked
                by a symphony
                        of childhood joy.
                                        Screams
and laughter
                of terrific together times
                                spun through the dimming
day and
        the sinking sun.
                        And all too soon,
                                the moment's gone,
reduced to wet feet
                and stinging digits
                                and doors closing
and hot chocolate
                and up the stairs
                        and off to bed   and soft
as snow:
            Goodnight   *Goodnight*   *Goodnight*

behold! the star tent of the universe

the great cathedral sky

breathe deep your oneness with the world

for this, then, is its promise

night and a new day

you are here

and so am I

                                   & it is the wish of wings
to fly

                                      so fly

                                  so fly

                              so fly

I once was forgotten, lonely, lost
Yet still quite alive beneath time's frost
You found me, spellbound me, warmed me through
Now I am a phoenix: blazing and new

And So It Begins
Not A Whimper But A Bang
Heartbeat Number One

Verses from the Time of Treacle

In Costa Del Back Garden

In Costa Del Back Garden
your local camping site,
there's so much to see and do,
a weekend of delight.

In Costa Del Back Garden
you only need a tent,
a sleeping bag and pillow
for your holiday event.

In Costa Del Back Garden
you'll see birds and buzzing bees
and worms and giant beetles.
Take a picture: smile, cheese!

In Costa Del Back Garden
the trees and plants and flowers
will bend and sway and bloom and play
and entertain your eyes for hours.

In Costa Del Back Garden
you can party with your friends,
explorers of the undergrowth
that make-believe extends.

In Costa Del Back Garden
you can build a secret den
deep in the darkest branches,
just like they did back then.

In Costa Del Back Garden
the sun's not guaranteed,
but once it's here, it's awf'y good,
on this we're all agreed.

In Costa Del Back Garden
there are no water rides,
but if you've got some water guns
then you could improvise.

In Costa Del Back Garden
if there's ever too much mud,
your house is but a step away.
(Please flee there in a flood.)

In Costa Del Back Garden
when nature comes to call,
don't fret or sweat or panic;
the toilet's down the hall.

In Costa Del Back Garden
the food is good, it's true.
The smell comes wafting from the grill
of the greasy barbecue.

In Costa Del Back Garden
you can sing songs round the fire,
and toast some pink marshmallows
till to bed you must retire.

In Costa Del Back Garden
you can sleep beneath the stars
with the lullaby of whistling wind
and the roll of distant cars.

In Costa Del Back Garden
one really mustn't snore.
Please don't disturb the neighbours:
they're sound-averse next door.

In Costa Del Back Garden
you can dream of soon-to-bes,
cradled in the canvas
beneath the watchful trees.

In Costa Del Back Garden
there's so much to do and see:
a memory-filled staycation,
and best of all it's free!

Yes, Costa Del Back Garden,
the best resort in town,
is waiting just beyond your door.
Grab a tent and peg it down.

When We Heard 2020

When we heard 2020, we used to think of vision,
we used to think of clarity, of seeing with precision.
We didn't know back then, of course, that in this year of years,
the world would fill our eyes but also fill our ears
with a cacophony of sound effects from very small to great:
the soundtrack to a striking year which I'll now elucidate.

It started with the sound of words, newly-built, unmet,
but they seemed so far away they couldn't possibly pose a threat;
then came voices of reporters, saying something could be coming;
then water cooler whispers tried to drown the future's humming;
then came sirens of confusion, of panic, of fear,
for the noise that once was distant was closer, closer, here.

It was the sound of numbers and they didn't seem to pause,
and the theatres all went silent, ending their applause,
and the school bells stopped their ringing, pubs gave their last last
   orders,
and the skies gave up the sound of planes as the world closed
   down its borders,
and thus the great machine seized up, with all its engines ceasing,
and in the silence came the counting of the numbers still
   increasing . . . . .

But also in the silence, there came the sound of hope
as communities came together and together learned to cope:
with kinder words and helping hands and new-formed ways to
   shop;
new teachers used their teacher-voice, and also prepared to hop

to the sound of PE on TV with running, jumping, crawling;
with the "Yas!!!" of online quizzing; and families virtually calling,

with the "—Hello!—
                    —Can you hear me?—
                                —Can you see me?—
                                            —Oh!—Hello!—Hi!—",
and the "—Okay!—
                    —Catch you soon!—
                                —Now how d'you turn it—?—
                                            —Okay!—Goodbye!—";
and the gardens blazed with wildlife, all nature could be heard,
and if you listened closely, the song of a newborn bird;
and the click-clack of a walking frame from a guy who didn't want
        a fuss,
to the sound of saluting sky-planes saying, "Happy Birthday,
        Captain Tom, from us!";

and the chorus of our Thursday nights when the nation did
        express
gratitude to front line staff, when we clapped for the NHS;
aye, we clapped for our key workers, but then we stopped, you see,
because they didn't need a clap, they needed PPE;
and somewhere in the constant dance of daily truth and lies,
we formed a weird obsession with Dominic Cummings' eyes;

and that brings us to the laughter and the ones who made us roar;
in the dark, they found the light, and gave us gems like, "Frank, get
        the door!";

and in lieu of graduation, of celebrating school achievers,
our ears were blessed with the memories and melodies of
        a cappella songs of leavers.
But if there was a single sound that caused the world to seethe,
it was the eight minutes and forty-six seconds of "I can't breathe."

. . . and from its subsequent silence came the voices and each letter
spelt a clear instruction: we must make the future better.
It cannot sound like yesterday, and if we make our noise today,
we'll demonstrate to those who doubt there is a fairer way.
In each of us is music, an instrument of our own,
and when we play together, no-one plays alone.

Let 2020 be the year when our symphony is heard,
when the orchestra of humanity unites and the lines between are
        blurred,
and finally we'll hear the sound that we can't wait to hear,
the one I think we're waiting for, each and every ear:
it's the sound a body makes when being hugged so tightly,
and we'll each embrace the other, saying,
        "You are loved.
            You are loved.
                You are loved,
                    quite rightly."

There's no question that this year of note was filled with sounds
        aplenty,
but which will we remember as the sound of 2020?

There's No New Christmas Songs This Year

there's no new Christmas songs this year
there's no new party games to play
there's no new cracker jokes to hear
and no new mistletoe bouquet

there's no new programmes on our tellies
no new adverts to endure
there's no new socks and no new smellies
no new snow so soft and pure

there's no new trimmings on the tables
no new warm and crisp mince pies
there's no new cosy bedtime fables
no new stars a-sweeping skies

there's no new presents to unwrap
there's no new lights or trees to dress
there's no new pantomimes to clap
there's no new Christmas, well, unless

unless there are new songs to sing
as yet unwritten, still in here
there is a warmth that words can bring
this winter and throughout the year

these are the Christmas songs we'll write
through conversation, simple talk
it isn't much, it may seem slight
but even beans can sprout a stalk

the gesture may not seem so huge
but tiny lamps still cast a light
as transformation splendoured Scrooge
we will ride out this darkest night

there'll be new Christmas songs this year
the ones composed from what we say
when we tell folk who need to hear
that they are loved this winter day

Counting in Years

2019

Each time we spoke the year aloud
we invoked a secret countdown:
twenty, nineteen.
But we didn't hear the tick.
We didn't know the fuse was lit,
and chose instead to dance and party on,
our future rearing in like Hogmanay,
the seconds slipping, voices clipping:
ten, nine, eight, seven, six, five, four,
three, two, one, gone.

2020

Each time we spoke the year aloud
we stuttered on the stuckness:
twenty, twenty.
Like a bad dream
whose grip you cannot shake,
we were ambered yearners trekking
through treacle, barriered from people,
future retreating, voices repeating:
twenty, twenty, twenty, twenty,
twenty, twenty, twenty, empty.

2021

Each time we speak the year aloud
we'll remind ourselves of rising:
twenty, twenty-one.
The path will not be easy, twenty, twenty-one,
we can't go over it, can't go under it, we've got to go
through it, twenty, twenty-one, together,
step by step, mountain by mountain,
constantly countin', twenty, twenty-one,
up and up, hope reignited, voices united:
twenty, twenty-one, and on!

Everychild vs. the Time of Treacle

Let me tell you of Everychild,
of how they lived through the Time of Treacle
when all was stuck and sticky in the world.

Let me tell you how they loved chocolate and cakes
and waffles and juice, how the smell of apple crumble
could pull them through a house;
how they loved animals, their pets, like dogs and horses,
and those of greater distance, like pandas and sharks;
how they loved their bikes and the chance to explore
the world around them; how they laughed at jokes,
and travelled through screens and the pages of books;
of the freckles on their face,
and the blue-nosed teddy in their arms;
let me tell of the saxophone they were learning to play;
their insatiable love of tractors;
and how they dug deep in their mind
to find the words of this poem.

Let me tell you how Everychild
remembered when the Time of Treacle hadn't yet arrived,
when they could do what they wanted;
when they used to go to football games
and play in rugby tournaments with their friends;
how they felt when they bought their first pack
of trading cards, and watched the first film
in a now-favourite series; how they felt
when they didn't like riding their bike,
but kept pedalling towards the future anyway;

and when they ran sun-soaked
through the fountains in Malta,
the memory of that water now forever on their skin.

Let me tell you what Everychild
wanted the future to know, starting with this:
don't fall off your bike, it hurts;
strawberries are pretty good,
but mint choc chip is the superior ice-cream flavour;
climate change is a big deal, but flying cars are a bad idea;
the way to get things started
is to quit talking and start doing;
you only have one life, don't waste it;
don't litter, leave only love;
and if you do fall off your bike,
get back on, and keep pedalling.

And let me end by telling you what Everychild
wished for in that terrible Time of Treacle:
they wished for adventures,
a journey to the jungle, or cage diving with the sharks;
they wished for fun with friends;
they wished to be a doctor, to help people;
to entertain, by playing their saxophone
for all the world to hear;
they wished for a big, shiny, real, red tractor,
to drive around the fields all day,
they wished for better stationery
with which to fashion better poems;

and finally they wished for apple crumble,
for its smell of home to pull them through the wild.

This was the story of Everychild,
of how they lived through the Time of Treacle
when all was stuck and sticky in the world.

In Costa Del Back Garden — Reprise

Remember when we summered here
in tents beneath that sky so clear,
with sunlight streaming – belvedere! –
      in Costa Del Back Garden.

Remember who we were back then:
the great explorers of the den
we built ourselves. Let's roam again
      through Costa Del Back Garden.

Remember what we used to play,
those games from dawn till bed of day,
when stars would plant themselves and say,
      sweet dreams, Costa Del Back Garden.

Remember how we'd place our palms
upon the earth, reciting charms,
that Nature would enfold her arms
      round Costa Del Back Garden.

Remember where that garden grew
and where it grows: it grows in you,
as childhood is wont to do —
      bloom, Costa Del Back Garden!

Snake Eye to a Half Midnight

I don't know about you, but it often seems to me that Future is just Chance decked out in a different guise, our lives welcoming these costumed prospectors to play with us, advancing in some way our great game. So, I invite you to indulge me: go and grab a die. Just a normal one, six faces. Go on. I'll wait.

// ... //

Thank you. Now roll it, and let chance choose your future, as it so often has chosen mine.

■

Dice have been used since before recorded history, but their exact point of origin remains uncertain.

I've always been me, as long as *me* has been here, but the lack of a definitive source-point label led to the inquisition of my youth, the oft-repeated question: "If there's a football match between Scotland and England, who would you support?" Back then, I'd panic and babble my way out of the corner, knowing that my honest answer would only cause further resentment and alienation. Now, though, I won't even entertain the notion that I have to choose one over the other. What's important now is not where I'm from, but rather, where I'm going — and it's not as if I'm going to a football match any time soon. After all, back then, the honest answer was that I couldn't care less about football.

⊡

The faces of a traditional cubed die are marked with different numbers of pips, from one to six, with opposite sides summing to seven.

During my teens, I became obsessed with the stage, always acting and writing and listening to musical theatre cast albums on a loop — and so it was only natural when it came to choosing a university course that I would end up studying mathematics. Because who doesn't love a good plot twist, eh? Despite making it through the degree (and I do want you to know that my final-year one-man mathematical stand-up comedy routine is still talked about to this day), maths never sated me. The regret of following that supposedly safer path, however, did eventually teach me the importance of directing my own show, my own life, in my own way. Our days are numbered, but there is no script. Tomorrow is unwritten, and I will never sum to seven.

⚁

Certain dice, such as those used in casinos, have their pips drilled, then filled with a paint of the same density as the material used for the dice, to ensure that the centre of gravity of the dice is as close to the geometric centre as possible; in this way, concerns that the pips will cause a small bias are allayed.

— but what if chance would have it that some of our hollow parts were filled with words of greater weight? — and what if each letter of each word pulled us decisionways into a throw not of our own casting? What then, I ask you? What then? For I was thrown like this, tossed, debilitated into what I thought was another today, but realise now to have been merely a moment from a passing yesterday, drowning in a sea of *Why?*, the odds ever against me. — . . . and what if I knew that the future would drill away those words and fill me, instead, with me? — I would smile. — and dream.

⚃

On some dice, the single pip is a colourless depression.

No, I will not remember days spent frozen-trapped on the duvet, the sun sailing past, above me, beyond me. Nor will I remember the empty streets, how the crescent cried a lullaby each time I toed its lips. Or the loneliness of being the only person in the pub, tureen of soup for one, happy birthday to me. No, I will not remember those things. Instead, I'll sift their grey silt, pan their alluvium for golden flashes, however small, and fashion a pair of phoenix wings, crimson, burnt orange, ready to take flight into bluest sky, the sun sailing on, beside me, within me.

⬚

Multiple pigments may be added during the manufacturing process, resulting in the creation of a speckled or marbled die.

There will come a day in the vast, unknowable futuretimes when I meet him. I imagine it will happen outside, simply so the sky can soundtrack the scene, that calm note the air makes when the universe creaks. I think we'll be wearing the same clothes, the same shoes, the same nervous smile. We will be essentially the same person, but different. He will be me and I will be him. He will say to me, *Thank you*, and I will say to him, *Was it worth it?*, and he will lean in close, kiss me, and reply, *Only one way to find out*, and at last the die will be cast.

The word die comes from Old French, dé; from Latin, datum — "something which is given or played".

The greatest gift I've ever been given is a clock, embedded in a curve of glass, upon which the gifter inscribed a message both simple and moving. The words of that message and the mechanism's tick-tock remind me not only that the past exists, but also that the future is coming — and I say, finally, Bring. It. On. With all its summer warmth and fiery storms, bring it on. With all its cloudy days and star-filled skies, bring it on. With all its laughter and its love, with its smiling crescents and phoenix feathers, with its music and numbers and words and wonders, with its coming-soons and yet-to-bes, with its wide-open arms of acceptance and the chance to change, I say, bring it on. Bring on life. Because the future has promised me, It's time to play — and you no longer need the die.

Poems for a Year of Coasts and Waters

Coasts & Waters: **Prelude**

Come, set your ear by the water's spring
and hear it sing of river, rock pool, ocean,
still yourself from motion, taking time to hear its call:
    the water's flow connects us all.

Crab: **The Nightwatchman of the Shore**

Beyond the gentle lapping of the crisp evening's foam,
the nightwatchman wakes:
it's Deputy Decapod, claw of the law, with a beach to comb.

She scuttles by the shoreline with its faintly drifting flakes,
with its lullabying lull,
ah, beautiful, and then – as ever – a battle plan she makes.

First, she scans the evidence already searched by PC Gull:
a twist of silver wrapping
left by picnickers, *typical,* and that she's been left to cull;

then a tin that if not taken could be dangerously entrapping;
and other snares from summertime;
then the ruins of a plaintive palace with its flag still flapping:

a once great sandcastle (early afternoon, they say, was its prime)
sent crumbling by all-aged youth —
and now she sets the punishment that best befits the crime.

It does not take a clever crab to be this moment's sleuth:
the humans are to blame
with their "beach-is-ours" mentality, so coarse and so uncouth.

She shakes serrated claws and vows to nip the human name,
then, defeated, scuttles home,
knowing that tomorrow's beat will be beaten just the same.

Dolphin: **Seven Sightings of the Noble Cetacean**

See a steel rainbow arc the sky from sea to sea.
Trace a hoary question mark in space beyond the quay.

> Fast. Noble. Loyal. True.
> Dolphin does as dolphins do.

Eye a blunt torpedo run beneath the foamy firth.
Track a flick of fin and fun outrun by gloaming's berth.

> Fast. Noble. Loyal. True.
> Dolphin does as dolphins do.

Spot a sickle silver moon aboon the seventh wave.
Mark a smidge of pearly bridge, and spy a scaled stave.

> Fast. Noble. Loyal. True.
> Dolphin does as dolphins do.

Dragonflies: **Overheard on the Swinston Ponds**

O Nymph—O Nymph—O are you prepared?
Today's your day. Don't be scared.

> O Poet—O Poet—O what do you mean?
> I am not scared in my pond so green.

O Nymph—O Nymph—O are you prepared?
For all that you'll be is soon to be aired.

> O Poet—O Poet—O what do you mean?
> I'm something more than all I've been?

O Nymph—O Nymph—O are you prepared?
There's more to you than what you've shared.

> O Poet—O Poet—O what do you mean?
> What is this future that you've seen?

O Nymph—O Nymph—O are you prepared?
You'll fly and you'll flash as Nature declared!

> O Poet—O Poet—O what do you mean?
> You have the wrong nymph—but what is this sheen?

Eels: **Song of the Elongated Lemniscates**

We are
resident of river and dweller of ditch and citizen of silt.
We are
burnished bronze and oily olive and slip-quick silver.
We are
water worm and sea snake and ocean oscillation.
We are
double helix and infinity and double helix.
We are
ocean oscillation and sea snake and water worm.
We are
slip-quick silver and oily olive and burnished bronze.
We are
citizen of silt and dweller of ditch and resident of river.

Frog: The Little Prince in Green

Like you, we leap from pad to pad,
from page to page, as poets
passing through —

Like you, we are the quiet ones,
sought for dissection,
prodded, prized —

Like you, we do not drink the world;
we absorb it through our skin
by noticing, noticing —

Like you, we are transformed by the press of lips
when our secret selves hop forth
from croak to crown —

Like you, we cannot tame our ripples
on the pool, and so instead
we enjoy the splash.

Grey Heron: **The Ashy Bird Amid the Algae's Throw**

At the pond, the grey heron is poised for the dip,
the blink-and-you'll-miss-it precision of lunch down the gullet.
Surreptitious-stander, you'd be forgiven
for not seeing on first glance the ashy bird amid the algae's throw,
but the heron is a waiter, most patient of diners,
master of statues and shadows and snap-snap-snap-and-gone.

Once, we were kids, here, at the pond, poised
to learn of nature's ways, the slow unfolding of the universe.
Spongy-ponderers, we were, keen
to get our mitts on wild things like slippery fish and flappy bats,
not owl pellets and regurgitations of the past,
and in the great impatience of what comes next,
perhaps we missed the lesson that life is snap-snap-snap and gone.

Kraken: **Ascension of the Ancient One**

Upon the soundless sunlit sea, a single ship:
a galley worked by many hands, and slickly so,
as though forever hence those hands would work the trip;
yet Fate – for reasons of her own – stirred up below.
For all on deck the day was just a day, no more,
no note of Revelation till – *ay!* – the world was split
by tow'ring tendril columns bursting out of it:
a hundred thick and writhing arms about a maw
that feasted on the cries of "Kraken!" *Hell was free!*
though naught but Hell itself could sate the ancient beast
and Hell it got as limb from limb it tore the tree
that birthed the boat and wrecked the hands that wrought the trip
till not one single grain remained and thus the ship
was lost. The kraken slipped beneath. The world uncreased,
and all was left was this: a soundless sunlit sea.

Mermaid: O! If Ye Be a Sailor

O! If ye be a sailor out a-sailing on the sea,
beware the song that does belong to mermaids or you'll be
a sorry, soggy sailor with a sorry, soggy fate
who'll wish they'd heeded unimpeded all I did relate.

O! If ye be a sailor out a-sailing on the sea,
beware the tune would make you swoon or else you're soon to be
a sorry, soggy sailor with a sorry, soggy fate
who'll wish they'd heeded unimpeded all I did relate.

O! If ye be a sailor out a-sailing on the sea,
beware the air so fine and fair as goss'mer hair or be
a sorry, soggy sailor with a sorry, soggy fate
who'll wish they'd heeded unimpeded all I did relate.

O! If ye be a sailor out a-sailing on the sea,
beware the ditty oh-so-pretty or you're bound to be
a sorry, soggy sailor with a sorry, soggy fate
who'll wish they'd heeded unimpeded all I did relate.

O! If ye be a sailor out a-sailing on the sea,
beware the sonnet, woah, be gone, it means you're gonna be
a sorry, soggy sailor with a sorry, soggy fate
who'll wish they'd heeded unimpeded all I did relate.

O! If ye be a sailor out a-sailing on the sea,
beware the song that does belong to mermaids or you'll be
a sorry, soggy sailor with a sorry, soggy fate
who'll wish they'd heeded unimpeded all I did relate.

Pond Skater: **Oarbug of the Millpond**

How I marvel at the miracle of you, pond skater!

How I goggle at your meticulous mechanics, pond skeeter!

How I admire grace in one so small, pond skipper!

How I gape to see you dodgem on the film, pond scooter!

How I wonder how you do it, pond skimmer!

How I dare to dream of walking water, pond strider!

Seahorse: **Sea Hook**

Contemplate the seahorse:
Lilliputian water dragon;
titchy paper lantern.

Sea Monster: A Carrick Encounter

To stand upon that precipice above the great abyss
with life rayed out before you to the sea and sky's far kiss
is all to say there's hope out there and sweetened air is bliss.

Just once, and long ago, I stood upon that very rock,
so green, and being young of course I heeded not the clock
till walls of yellow fog bloomed out the view; then, taking stock
of such a scene of silent gloom, it caught me by surprise
when through the murk emerged a pair of piercing saucer eyes
that lit upon my smaller self as though they'd found their prize.
A face came next, a snake-like face, a scaly floating wedge
with horns and fangs that cut the air, and I upon my ledge
for some compulsive reason stepped towards the very edge.
The hanging stare, mesmeric, of that serpent scrutineer
drew closer in but its intent remained as yet unclear.
I had the queerest feeling but the feeling wasn't fear;
the feeling was acknowledgement, accepting that it's true
that though the sea is full of hope, the sea holds monsters too,
and with that thought I nodded and the monster then withdrew.
The sea is deep, the sea is wide, and monsters lurk within,
but knowing there are battles that we never have to win
is just enough to give us strength to take the first step in.

When next I met the monster, some years later, all at sea,
I stared upon the monster and the monster stared at me,
and that was that, for this is life, and monsters, here they be.

Selkie: **Beltane on the Beach**

It was Beltane on the beach and the night fires burned,
that night when the selkies came ashore.

New crimson gallantly licked the salt of the stars,
and silver skins were stowed in hearths,
that night when the selkies came ashore.

Old tales were passed and polished from hand to hand,
and the old songs were sung, old dances were danced,
and all souls were blessed from first note till last,
that night when the selkies came ashore.

Cooried in, they sat watching the renewal of earth,
and the selkies and the humans were free from all fear,
and they treated each other with the greatest of care,
and no-one was sealed to the person they were,
that night when the selkies came ashore.

That night, selkie and human were one and the same,
till the people dispersed up spidering lanes,
till the cavernous undersea welcomed its own,
till the clocks over hearths called forth a new dawn,
as Fire and Water spun silver from air,
that night when the selkies came ashore.

Shells: **A Sketchbook**

The periwinkle shell is a porcelain vortex,
a brief whirlpool of the ocean's eye.

The limpet shell is an identified flying saucer,
grounded, a magnificent minute mountain.

The whelk shell is a bulbous helter-skelter,
grainy meringue whipped to a finish.

The mussel shell is an earlobe in oils,
the shoreline's inky teardrop.

The cockle shell is a rail schematic
with curved tracks for tiny aquatic trains.

The scallop shell is an elegant fan,
theatre footlight of a sculptured sunrise.

The razor shell is a brittle-bad banana peel,
bamboo sheath and shined drainpipe.

The conch shell is a spinning top, split
and splaying into the fourth dimension.

Starfish: **Sunbather**

Pinwheel of the rock pool, the starfish sits in its glassy world,
flexing mussels, its flesh the salmony orange of a setting sky.
Loss of limb? No problem. It has mastered regeneration.
Loss of friend or family member? No problem.
It stargazes on a clear night.

Swan: The Bird of Parnassus

A perfect folded napkin on the pond,
the swan.

A writer's muse, the first blank page,
the swan.

A turning of white curves, plumped,
the swan.

A fairy tale and beautiful since birth,
the swan.

A half of love to be sung at the edge,
the swan.

A graceful sky-set V, pointing ever on,
the swan.

Coasts & Waters: **Coda**

Come, set your ear by the river's surge
and hear it urge your eyes to look with wonder
on its skin and under, taking time to stop and see:
see the ashy bird a-waiting, standing poised and contemplating;
see the nymphs as they aspire to breathe out the dragon's fire;
see the lemniscating eels; see how water-walking feels;
see the swan, a perfect folding; see the little prince a-golding;
      the water's flow connects us all, drink deep.

Come, set your ear by the rock pool's rim
and hear it brim with whispers for the telling,
eye its sandy dwelling, taking time to stop and see:
see the starfish flexing mussels in its slow-mo action tussles;
see the crab perform its duty; see the selkies in their beauty
round the fire silver-spinning ancient songs from their beginning;
see the shells and count their number, trickle into dreamy slumber;
      the water's flow connects us all, drink deep, drink deep.

Come, set your ear by the ocean's core
and hear it roar of big blue worlds a-teeming,
watch with eyes a-gleaming, taking time to stop and see:
see the sea hook's spiral tail; see the mermaid's fatal scale;
see the kraken's mythic blow; see the dolphin's archer's bow;
and if you reach the water's edge, recall the water monster's pledge
to see yourself reflected, returned and reconnected;
      the water's flow connects us all, drink deep, drink deep, drink deep.

Quintet

On Poet's Path

The morning thistle cracks the planet's skin,
and Poet ploughs a furrow in the earth:
a flash of red emerges from within,
  with words as witness to a vulpine birth.

This chieftain runs where other foxes ran,
through legacy begat at Poet's house:
where else, but writ, could mouse become a man,
  and, by extension, man become a mouse?

The path extends from den to death and on,
where, finding freedom, fox gives way to fox.
With liberty regained, the flash is gone,
  and *who shall be our poet now?*
         The clocks

  are chiming. Here's the passing of a pen.
  The Earth spins on. The path begins, again.

The Working Birds

We watched as blue tits built their nest
this spring within our garden, blessed
to sit as architecture's guest
        from dawn till gloam,
as day by day they strived and stressed
        to build a home.

They worked with unrelenting zest
to find and fetch and craft their best,
till king and queen puffed-up a chest:
        Now we belong.
They paid to be our garden's guest
        with nowt but song.

With that, we thought the tits would rest,
but one kept zipping on a quest:
a feathered streak, a bird possessed.
        We knew the score:
what once had been a two-bird nest
        would soon be more.

And sure enough, as we had guessed,
the space within the box compressed,
when sharp and shrill and unrepressed
        new songs were sung
that split the sky, the silence wrest:
        the cry of young.

Such to- and fro-ing from the nest
left us breathless and impressed
to watch the parents' greatest test:
        to raise their own.
Another morsel to digest
        atop our throne.

The weeks slid by and we addressed
a sadness we could both attest
that soon we'd host an empty nest,
        sans songs, sans birds.
The parting of the ways was pressed
        in air, in words.

And on the day they flew the nest,
we felt a tugging in our chest,
as bird by bird, they bravely blessed
        our patch of blue:
first frenzied flight with helmet crest,
        then gone. Like you.

This autumn, now, we sit and rest
in silence, in an empty nest.
Not sad, just hoping for the best
        for you, our world.
Go fly like blue tits, proudly dressed
        with wings, unfurled.

The Memory of Water

Remember the time
when Greg the goldfish died, twice.

He went belly-up,
as with most precious things in life, but

your hands, soft
with age, raised him from the water.

You took him
from the very thing that brought him life

to give him life.
The backs of your fingers brushed his scales,

pushing death
out of his double-thumbnail body, gifting

a second chance
at life in a water-filled globe of glass. He lasts

for just one extra day,
but it is the best day, because Greg the goldfish

forgets how it feels
to die, and instead lives with the memory of water.

Notes for Pitching a Tent

First, choose a footprint of flat ground,
a vacant brush of earth upon which to limpet
your canvas shell to the face of the planet.
Check the ground for sticks and stones
and thorny names; remove them.
Clear the grass carpet as best you can.
Lay out the pieces that make the whole.
You know they are all there; you checked at home
and practised their putting-together.
Name them as you place them down:
canvas, skin; pole, backbone; peg,
earth-hook. Treat them with care.
You are building your tent not just for tonight
but tomorrow and tomorrow and tomorrow.
The air above your footprint is anticipatory.
It's as if it somehow knows that some of it will soon
be inside the impermanence of a pop-up home,
a future memory. It is, naturally, excited, like you.
This excitement is the wind; pitch in its direction,
door downhill if on a slope. Anchor
the back of the groundsheet to the ground,
and peg it loosely out, corners first, ensuring everything
is zipped. Push the poles into their positions,
their snug little tunnel adventures on the way into grass.
Do not force their journey. Give them the time
you required as you inched your way
through life. The poles are shock-corded.
Enjoy the sound of it all: the click of pole to connector,
pole to connector; togetherness clicking into place

on this tiny patch of the planet's skin.
Re-peg. Unravel the guy lines.
Allow them to follow the seams of the canvas.
Mallet them into the earth with pegs, forty-five degrees.
Coast your footprint's perimeter,
tightening, loosening, securing, as required.
Unzip, and welcome the world
into this newly-built speck of landscape.
Be satisfied with your work:
you took the pieces and brought them together.
Stand back and take notice of the other tents around you.
Campsite Earth is taking shape.
Help others erect their tents,
just as these notes helped you.
The dark is closing in. Night is upon us.
Act fast, but act well. See: the stars are arriving.
That sound? A song of hope, taking flight from a campfire.
We will be okay. We have pitched our tents for tomorrow,
trusting the earth to hold on to them tight.

After the Sky

As the dark hills above town turn themselves
into the cool plum of twilight —

As the burnt-out disc of orange sun is left behind
beyond the rising ridge —

As the silhouetted dandelion clocks of the wind farm rotate
towards the tenebrific hour —

As the slow parade of telegraph poles carry their drooping cables
through the air's empty lung —

As the last ghostly ruffles of vapour trails melt away to nothing
above the constant pull of the peaks —

As the first planet blinks into distant acknowledgement
next to a thin curl of moon —

As the night lays claim to an ending like the closing of a book —
a small voice sounds from a lit phone:

"It happens in more than one of your poems
but I like how Poet is elevated to magician
or master of the universe."

— and at that moment, up there, in the dark hills above town,
a pen starts to write and the universe creaks.

Notes on the Poems

CATHEDRAL SKY

This sequence was originally written as a poetic response to my experiences over the years of 2018 and 2019, and subsequently published as a pamphlet of the same name to accompany my tour that winter. Several entries grew out of creative writing workshops hosted by Fife-based writer Geoff Barker, and the penultimate verse (*I once was forgotten, lonely, lost*) was originally commissioned by Austrian carpenter Jakob Ofenberger for World Wood Day in 2019, inspired by its theme of Change, making something new from something old. Aside from some modifications to their layout on the page, the words of the sequence remain unedited from their first publication.

VERSES FROM THE TIME OF TREACLE

In Costa Del Back Garden

This first entry in my pandemic-themed poetry cycle began life as a community video project featuring thirty performers (and their gardens) from Scotland, England, Iceland and the Netherlands. I gratefully acknowledge all who gave their time and talents to the creation of the final product. It premiered on 20th August 2020.

When We Heard 2020

The theme of National Poetry Day in the UK in 2020 was Vision, and although the many new sights we saw that year were indeed something to behold, I responded to the theme with this poem inspired by the seemingly overlooked *sound* of lockdown. There are numerous references throughout the piece; I leave the reader to find naturally the sounds most meaningful to them. The video premiered on National Poetry Day, 1st October 2020.

There's No New Christmas Songs This Year

This poem was commissioned by the Wick Players, an amateur dramatics society based in Caithness of which I was a member for a number of years, as part of their advent calendar of festive digital releases. In it, I reference their recent winter productions, including nods to *Jack and the Beanstalk*, *A Christmas Carol* and *Aladdin*. It premiered on 15th December 2020.

Counting in Years

These verses grew out of a fragment written at the end of 2019 in which I wrote of the secret countdown I noticed was being uttered when the year was spoken aloud: twenty, nineteen. Who was to know, eh? Who was to know? Given how the following year unfolded, I expanded the original scribble into the full poem presented here. The video premiered with the turn of the year on New Year's Day, 1st January 2021.

Everychild vs. the Time of Treacle

This poem developed out of four workshops I delivered to the 2nd Lanark Cub Packs; I acknowledge the words and imagination of the young people in its creation. The accompanying video, featuring a lone voice over the stark visual of an abandoned play park, premiered on World Poetry Day, 21st March 2021.

In Costa Del Back Garden – Reprise

Concluding my pandemic-themed poetry cycle, this poem returns us to the No. 1 holiday destination of the lockdowns, taking us right back to the start with a musing on memories and childhood. The video premiered on 20th August 2021, exactly one year after the first visit to our Costa Del Back Gardens.

SNAKE EYE TO A HALF MIDNIGHT

Each year, the Scottish Book Trust runs an initiative called *Your Stories* in which members of the public are invited to write in any style, in a personal way, in response to a chosen theme. In 2020, the theme was Future, and this piece (something existing between the forms of poetry and short story) was my contribution. As a note of interest, my entry for 2021's theme of Celebration, *Friday Night Treat* – a poem about fish 'n' chips and all the other big little things in life – was chosen for publication in the annual physical book produced as part of the initiative, with 50,000 copies printed and available for free around the country during Book Week Scotland, 15th to 21st November 2021.

POEMS FOR A YEAR OF COASTS AND WATERS

This sequence of nature poems was inspired by Scotland's Year of Coasts and Waters 20/21, specifically the willow sculpture trail *Culzean by the Sea*, a series of fifteen bespoke pieces designed by Girvan-based sculptor David Powell, displayed around Culzean Castle and Country Park throughout the summer of 2021. As a child, I spent a wealth of happy weekends in the grounds of Culzean with the Young Naturalists' Club. In 2003, I won a competition to design the birthday cake for the group's 30th anniversary, prominently featuring their logo, the grey heron. That same bird features here, where I hope to have captured something of the rush of childhood and the still beauty of what it is to really *see*. The now-renamed Mini Rangers will celebrate their 50th anniversary in 2023. I dedicate this sequence to them with thanks for those green years in the trees.

QUINTET

On Poet's Path

In Alloway, Ayrshire, there is a short track to be found connecting Burns Cottage (the first home of Robert Burns) and the Robert Burns Birthplace Museum. The trail, known as Poet's Path, both spans and celebrates Burns' legacy, with specially commissioned pieces of art inspired by his work lining the way. I was honoured to be asked by the museum's resident Scots Scriever Tracy Harvey and Events Manager Lauren McKenzie to contribute a poem to their week of celebrating National Poetry Day in 2020, and it was irresistible to pen a verse on the aforementioned path. Poems referenced in the piece include *On Glenriddel's Fox Breaking His Chain* and *To a Mouse*, the latter in acknowledgement of the two metre tall version of the title creature as seen on the route. It premiered, as a video recorded on location, on 7th October 2020.

The Working Birds

This poem, a fictional narrative inspired by real blue tits, won the Robert Burns World Federation's international "Write A Habbie" poetry competition in 2021, Habbie being a recognisable six-line poetic verse form oft-employed by the Bard. The awarding was announced on Burns Day, 25th January 2021, during the RBWF's first virtual Burns Supper.

The Memory of Water

This poem, inspired by a personal memory, featured extensively in the creative writing workshops I delivered during 2021.

Notes for Pitching a Tent

After contributing a pre-existing poem to their first virtual international St George's Day event in 2020, Scoutadelic (the tireless Mike Rouse-Deane) commissioned a new piece from me on the themes of Togetherness and Hope for the 2021 event. A poetry prompt from Helena Nelson of HappenStance Press suggested the writing of instructions for an activity frequently carried out by the writer. This put me in mind of *Notes for Lighting a Fire* by Gerry Cambridge, one of my favourite poems from a favourite Scottish poet, to which I nod with my own title. The video, a personal favourite, premiered in Scoutadelic's event on 25th April 2021.

After the Sky

The cover of *When the Universe Creaks* was illustrated by Crewe-based graphic designer Jamie Steel, and, after falling in love with it, I wrote this poem in response as the finale to the book. The quote is real, taken verbatim from my best mate, Richard Smith. Interpretation, as is the way with all art, is left to the reader.

Acknowledgements

First, for their assistance and/or enthusiasm in the creation of the original *Cathedral Sky* pamphlet, I'd like to thank the following: Laura Stewart, Annie Dimond, Geoff Barker, Fiona McFadzean, George Cameron, Meghan Potter and Lindsay Littleson.

My grandmother, Joan Mills, is always waiting patiently by her phone, ready to hear each new poem as it is completed. Thanks, Nanna, for your constant support with my creative work. I'll forever cherish your wee gasps of joy whenever I finish reading a new poem to you; they mean so much to me.

I'm grateful to my parents, Jane and Nigel Lamb, for keen ears, honest feedback and other stuff. (P.S. Dad, cheers for all the filming!) (P.P.S. Sorry about your knotted pine.)

I owe a great debt to Jamie Steel for this book's beautiful cover, so perfectly tuned as it is to the poetry within. Jamie, you absolutely aced it. I hope you like the poem your art inspired.

Thanks, too, to Michelle Shepherd, Countryside Ranger at Culzean, for talking to me about the Young Naturalists' Club.

During the pandemic, I kindled an e-friendship with fellow poet Richard Bramwell. His endless encouragement and warm wit fire and inspire me with every new correspondence. *Lit!*

Finally, my heartfelt thanks go to Richard Smith who reads and analyses every poem I write as though lives are at stake, or at least a Higher English grade, and with whom I can discuss the whole creaking universe.

About the Poet

SIMON LAMB is a Scottish poet, performer and storyteller. With a background in education, he also works extensively in schools to ignite and inspire young learners. His "wise, warm and witty" debut collection of poetry "for ages 7 to 107" will be published in 2022 by Scallywag Press, with illustrations from the much-loved former Children's Laureate, Chris Riddell.

You can find out more by visiting Simon's website

www.simonlambcreative.co.uk

and by following him on social media:

Facebook & Instagram — *@SimonLambCreative*

Twitter & YouTube — *@approx21words*